Minnesota LYNX

by Luke Hanlon

Copyright © 2026 by Press Room Editions. All rights reserved. No part of this book may be used or reproduced in any manner whatsoever, including internet usage, without written permission from the copyright owner, except in the case of brief quotations embodied in critical articles and reviews.

Book design by Kate Liestman
Cover design by Kate Liestman

Photographs ©: Tony Gutierrez/AP Images, cover; Elsa/Getty Images Sport/Getty Images, 4, 7, 8; Mitchell Layton/Getty Images Sport/Getty Images, 10; John Spivey/AP Images, 13; Hannah Foslien/Getty Images Sport/Getty Images, 14, 16, 19; Kevork Djansezian/Getty Images Sport/Getty Images, 20; Leon Bennett/Getty Images Sport/Getty Images, 23; Sam Wasson/Getty Images Sport/Getty Images, 24; Sean D. Elliot/The Day/AP Images, 27; David Berding/Getty Images Sport/Getty Images, 29

Press Box Books, an imprint of Press Room Editions.

ISBN
979-8-89469-016-2 (library bound)
979-8-89469-029-2 (paperback)
979-8-89469-054-4 (epub)
979-8-89469-042-1 (hosted ebook)

Library of Congress Control Number: 2025931641

Distributed by North Star Editions, Inc.
2297 Waters Drive
Mendota Heights, MN 55120
www.northstareditions.com

Printed in the United States of America
082025

ABOUT THE AUTHOR

Luke Hanlon is a sportswriter and editor based in Minneapolis. He's written dozens of nonfiction sports books for kids and spends a lot of his free time watching his favorite Minnesota sports teams.

TABLE OF CONTENTS

CHAPTER 1
CLUTCH SHOTS   5

CHAPTER 2
COLD START   11

CHAPTER 3
BUILDING A DYNASTY   17

SUPERSTAR PROFILE
MAYA MOORE   22

CHAPTER 4
A NEW STAR   25

QUICK STATS   30
GLOSSARY   31
TO LEARN MORE   32
INDEX   32

CHAPTER 1

CLUTCH SHOTS

Courtney Williams's shot clanked off the rim. But her Minnesota Lynx teammate Alanna Smith rebounded the miss. With time running out, Smith passed back out to Williams. The guard caught the ball behind the three-point line. New York Liberty guard Sabrina Ionescu raced out toward Williams. Ionescu fouled

Sabrina Ionescu (20) fouls Courtney Williams late in Game 1 of the 2024 Finals.

Williams while she was shooting. However, the shot still swished home.

Only 5.5 seconds remained in Game 1 of the 2024 Women's National Basketball Association (WNBA) Finals. Williams's shot tied the score at 83–83. Then she made her free throw to put Minnesota up by one.

The Liberty still had enough time to win the game. They put the ball in Breanna Stewart's hands. The superstar forward drove hard to the basket. A Lynx defender fouled Stewart to stop her from scoring. If Stewart drained both free throws, the Liberty would win. But she made only one of them. So, the game went into overtime.

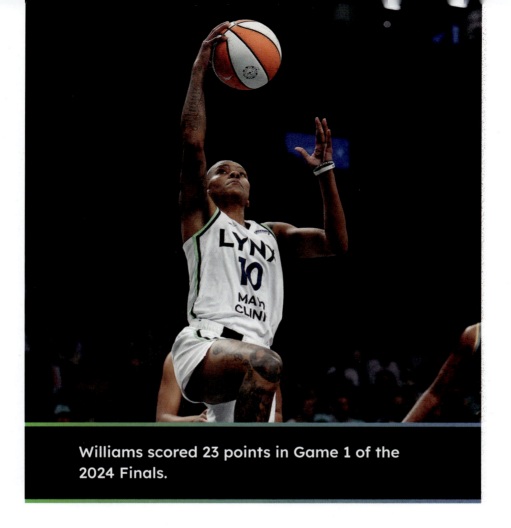

Williams scored 23 points in Game 1 of the 2024 Finals.

The two teams battled throughout the extra period. With 48 seconds left, Williams scored on a layup. That shot put the Lynx up by four. The Liberty refused to go down, though. They tied the game with 28 seconds left.

Napheesa Collier made both of her shot attempts in overtime of Game 1.

Minnesota had relied on Napheesa Collier for scoring all season. Game 1 was no different. With 14 seconds left, Williams bounced a pass to Collier in the paint. Liberty center Jonquel Jones defended Collier tightly. So, Collier dribbled back to the free-throw line. She stepped hard to her right. When Jones followed that move, Collier turned around for a jump shot. The ball went through the hoop with eight seconds remaining.

New York had one more chance to tie or win the game. Stewart darted toward the basket again. This time, she missed a layup at the buzzer. The crowd in New York fell silent as the Lynx celebrated a Game 1 win.

UNLIKELY WIN

The Liberty jumped out to an 18-point lead in the first half of Game 1. With five minutes left, the Liberty led 81–66. The Lynx then scored 18 of the game's next 20 points. By overcoming an 18-point deficit, Minnesota matched the largest comeback in WNBA Finals history.

CHAPTER 2

COLD START

The Minnesota Lynx joined the WNBA in 1999. Before their first season, they added Katie Smith. The guard quickly became Minnesota's best player. Smith could shoot from anywhere on the court. She scored the most points in the league in 2000 and 2001. She also played great defense. However, wins were hard to come by.

Katie Smith played in the All-Star Game five times with the Lynx.

The Lynx finished with a losing record in each of their first four seasons.

New coach Suzie McConnell-Serio helped turn things around. In 2003, she led the Lynx to their first playoff appearance. They faced the Los Angeles Sparks in the first round. The Sparks had won the championship the previous two years.

In Game 1, the Sparks showed off their playoff experience. Early in the second half, they led by 21 points. But the Lynx battled back. With 24 seconds left, Smith tied the game with a three-pointer. On the next possession, Tamika Williams stole an inbounds pass. Then the Lynx forward scored a game-winning layup. The crowd

Tamika Williams (20) averaged 6.7 points per game during her six seasons with Minnesota.

in Minnesota erupted to celebrate the team's first playoff win.

The good times didn't last, though. The Sparks won the next two games to take the series. The Lynx returned to the

Seimone Augustus was voted into the Basketball Hall of Fame in 2024.

playoffs in 2004. Once again, they lost in the first round.

Smith continued to play at a high level in 2005. But the Lynx struggled to win games. So, they traded Smith away. Minnesota finished the season with one of the league's worst records.

Those losses helped the Lynx receive the first pick in the 2006 draft. They used it on Seimone Augustus. The guard became one of the league's top scorers. Even so, the Lynx continued to struggle.

In 2010, Minnesota hired Cheryl Reeve as the team's new coach. The Lynx also traded for Minnesota native Lindsay Whalen that year. Soon, Reeve and Whalen would lead the Lynx to glory.

MASSIVE VICTORY

The Lynx won only 10 games in 2006. One of those wins came by a huge margin, though. Minnesota scored 114 points against the Los Angeles Sparks on May 31. The Lynx won the game by 43 points. That was the second-biggest winning margin in WNBA history.

CHAPTER 3

BUILDING A DYNASTY

The Lynx finished with a losing record in 2010. That marked their sixth straight losing season. However, Minnesota received the top pick in the 2011 draft. The Lynx picked Maya Moore.

Moore played well with Lindsay Whalen and Seimone Augustus. The trio led the Lynx back to the playoffs.

Maya Moore played in six All-Star Games during her career.

In the first round, Minnesota won a decisive Game 3. From there, the Lynx rolled through the playoffs. They swept the Phoenix Mercury in the semifinals. Then they swept the Atlanta Dream in the Finals. For the first time, the Lynx were WNBA champions!

Minnesota didn't slow down in 2012. The Lynx started the season on a 10-game win streak. They returned to the Finals. This time, the Indiana Fever won in four games. The loss didn't discourage the Lynx, though. They made it back to the playoffs in 2013. Once there, they didn't lose a single game. The Lynx swept the Dream in the Finals to win their second title.

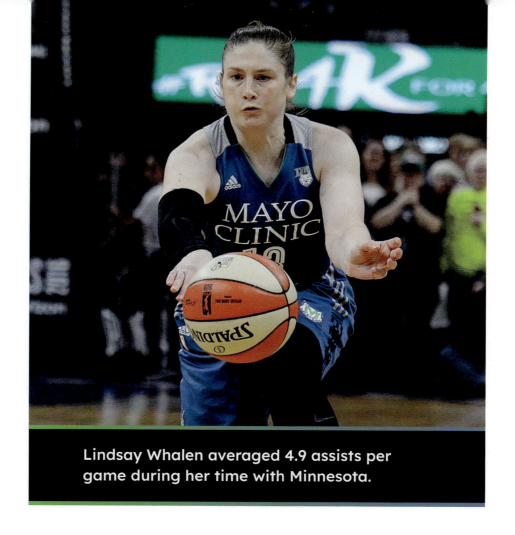

Lindsay Whalen averaged 4.9 assists per game during her time with Minnesota.

Making it to the semifinals would be a success for most teams. But not for the Lynx. They lost in the 2014 semifinals. So, the team made a big move in 2015. During that season, the Lynx traded for Sylvia Fowles.

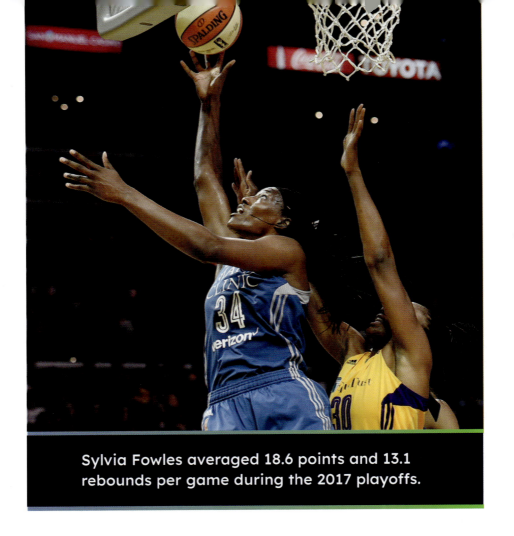

Sylvia Fowles averaged 18.6 points and 13.1 rebounds per game during the 2017 playoffs.

The Lynx made it back to the Finals in 2015. The Fever couldn't stop Fowles. She averaged 15.6 points and 9.4 rebounds per game. Fowles earned Finals Most Valuable Player (MVP) honors. And the Lynx secured their third title.

The Lynx were back in the Finals in 2016. They hosted Game 5. Minnesota led Los Angeles by one point as the clock ticked down. But with two seconds left, the Sparks hit a shot to win the title. The Lynx and Sparks had a rematch in the 2017 Finals. Once again, the series went to Game 5. This time, the Lynx came out on top. Minnesota secured its status as one the league's greatest dynasties.

BIGGER THAN BASKETBALL

Maya Moore took a break from basketball after the 2018 season. She wanted to help Jonathan Irons. He had been convicted of a crime. But Moore thought he was innocent. She worked to get Irons released from prison. In 2020, she succeeded. Moore never played in the WNBA again. She retired in 2023.

SUPERSTAR PROFILE

MAYA MOORE

Maya Moore rarely lost. In high school, she won 125 of 128 games. And she won three state titles. Moore played college ball at the University of Connecticut (UConn). The Huskies lost only four games in Moore's four years. She also helped UConn win two national championships.

Moore brought her winning ways to Minnesota. She earned Rookie of the Year honors in 2011. Then Moore lifted the Lynx to their first title. In her eight seasons, she led the Lynx to the Finals six times. And she never missed the playoffs.

Moore's scoring helped the Lynx win four titles. She averaged 18.4 points per game during her career. That average is the highest in team history. Her scoring almost always increased in the playoffs. In the 2013 Finals, Moore averaged 20 points per game. She earned Finals MVP honors for her performance.

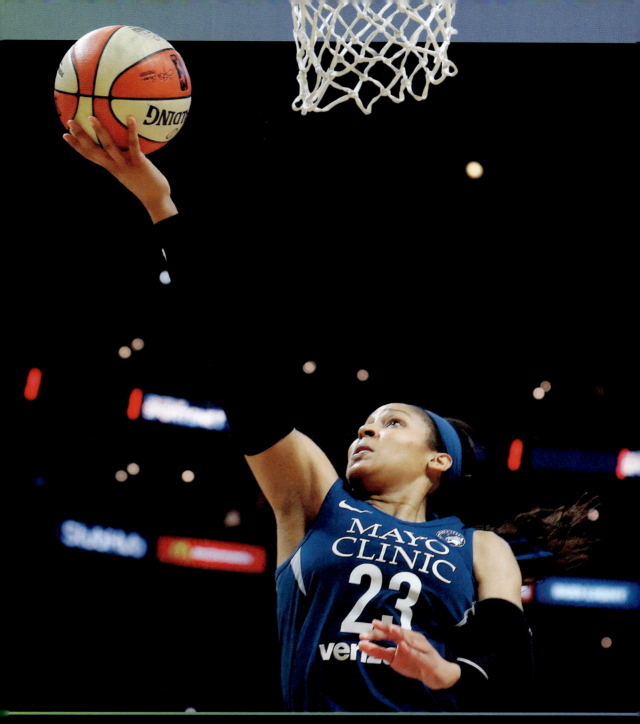

Moore made the All-WNBA First Team five times.

CHAPTER 4

A NEW STAR

Maya Moore left the Lynx after the 2018 season. Lindsay Whalen retired that year, too. In 2019, Seimone Augustus played her last season with Minnesota. The Lynx recovered quickly. They found a new star in the 2019 draft. Minnesota selected Napheesa Collier in the first round. The forward won Rookie of the

Napheesa Collier played in the All-Star Game as a rookie in 2019.

Year honors that season. Collier could take over games in the paint. She scored close to the basket. And she swatted away shots.

Collier and Sylvia Fowles kept the Lynx competitive. However, Minnesota lost in the first round of the playoffs in 2018 and 2019. The Lynx advanced to the semifinals in 2020. But the Seattle Storm swept the series.

Fowles decided 2022 would be her final season. Collier missed most of the year. She gave birth to her first child in May. At first, she planned to skip the entire season. But she sped up her recovery. She wanted to play with Fowles again before she retired. Collier returned in time to play

When Fowles retired in 2022, her 4,006 rebounds were in the most in WNBA history.

four games with Fowles. But the team had struggled without Collier. The Lynx missed the playoffs for the first time in 12 years.

The Lynx returned to the playoffs in 2023. However, they lost in the first round. Experts didn't expect much out of the Lynx in 2024. Cheryl Reeve believed in her team, though. The Lynx finished with one of the league's best records.

Minnesota faced the Connecticut Sun in the semifinals. The series went to Game 5. Collier recorded 27 points and 11 rebounds. She lifted the Lynx back to the Finals. There, they faced the New York Liberty.

A DIFFERENT CHAMPIONSHIP

The WNBA started the Commissioner's Cup in 2021. The tournament takes place during the regular season. In 2024, the Lynx faced the Liberty in the championship game. The Lynx won in New York 94–89. Each Minnesota player received up to $30,000 for the victory.

Collier won the Defensive Player of the Year Award in 2024.

Each game came down to the wire. Game 5 even went to overtime. In the end, the Liberty won. Still, fans in Minnesota believed their team was close to another title.

QUICK STATS

MINNESOTA LYNX

Founded: 1999

Championships: 4 (2011, 2013, 2015, 2017)

Key coaches:
- Brian Agler (1999–2002): 48–67
- Suzie McConnell-Serio (2003–06): 58–67, 1–4 playoffs
- Cheryl Reeve (2010–): 330–180, 49–28 playoffs, 4 WNBA titles

Most career points: Seimone Augustus (5,881)

Most career assists: Lindsay Whalen (1,381)

Most career rebounds: Sylvia Fowles (2,174)

Most career blocks: Sylvia Fowles (345)

Most career steals: Maya Moore (451)

Stats are accurate through the 2024 season.

GLOSSARY

decisive
Able to decide a winner.

draft
An event that allows teams to choose new players coming into the league.

dynasties
Teams that have an extended period of success, usually winning multiple championships in the process.

layup
An easy shot made close to the basket.

margin
The difference in points between the winner and loser.

overtime
An additional period of play to decide a game's winner.

paint
The area between the basket and the free-throw line.

retired
Ended one's career.

rookie
A first-year player.

swept
Won all the games in a series.

TO LEARN MORE

Berglund, Bruce. *Basketball GOATs: The Greatest Athletes of All Time*. Capstone Press, 2022.

O'Neal, Ciara. *The WNBA Finals*. Apex Editions, 2023.

Whiting, Jim. *The Story of the Minnesota Lynx*. Creative Education, 2024.

MORE INFORMATION

To learn more about the Minnesota Lynx, go to **pressboxbooks.com/AllAccess**. These links are routinely monitored and updated to provide the most current information available.

INDEX

Atlanta Dream, 18
Augustus, Seimone, 15, 17, 25

Collier, Napheesa, 8-9, 25-28
Connecticut Sun, 28

Fowles, Sylvia, 19-20, 26-27

Indiana Fever, 18, 20
Ionescu, Sabrina, 5-6
Irons, Jonathan, 21

Jones, Jonquel, 8-9

Los Angeles Sparks, 12-13, 15, 21

McConnell-Serio, Suzie, 12
Moore, Maya, 17, 21, 22, 25

New York Liberty, 5-9, 28-29

Phoenix Mercury, 18

Reeve, Cheryl, 15, 28

Seattle Storm, 26
Smith, Alanna, 5
Smith, Katie, 11-12, 14
Stewart, Breanna, 6, 9

Whalen, Lindsay, 15, 17, 25
Williams, Courtney, 5-8
Williams, Tamika, 12